An *Obergefreiter* of the *Luftwaffe* ground crew helps *Leutnant* Wolfgang Ziese, of *Kommando* Sperling, into the small cockpit of his photo-reconnaissance plane. Other small operational reconnaissance units were set up in 1944, including *Kommando* Hecht, activated on 10 November 1944 at Biblis not far from Worms-am-Rhein.

LUFTWAFFE AT WAR

German Jets
1944–1945

Manfred Griehl

Greenhill Books
LONDON

Stackpole Books
PENNSYLVANIA

Greenhill Books

German Jets, 1944–1945
first published 1999
by Greenhill Books, Lionel Leventhal Limited,
Park House, 1 Russell Gardens,
London NW11 9NN
www.greenhillbooks.com
and
Stackpole Books, 5067 Ritter Road, Mechanicsburg,
PA 17055, USA

© Lionel Leventhal Limited, 1999
The moral right of the author has been asserted.

British Library Cataloguing in Publication Data
Griehl, Manfred
German jets. - (Luftwaffe at war ; v. 10)
1.Germany. Luftwaffe - Equipment 2.Jet bombers -
Germany - History 3.Fighter planes - Germany - History 4.World War, 1939-1945 - Aerial operations, German
I.Title
623.7'46'044'0943'09044

ISBN 1-85367-356-0

Library of Congress Cataloging-in-Publication Data
Griehl, Manfred.
German jets / by Manfred Griehl.
    p.   cm. — (Luftwaffe at war ; v. 10)
ISBN 1-85367-356-0
1. Jet planes, Military—Germany. 2. World War, 1939-
1945—Aerial operations, German. I. Title. II. Series.
UG1245.G4G7538 1999
623.7'46044'094309044—dc21   98-49437
                                                 CIP

Designed by DAG Publications Ltd
Designed by David Gibbons
Layout by Anthony A. Evans
Printed in Singapore

LUFTWAFFE AT WAR
GERMAN JETS, 1944–1945

The jet aircraft was hailed as Germany's best chance of turning round a lost war, at a time when Allied armies were already on German soil, fighting in what – to them – was clearly a devastated country. The advent of jet-propelled aircraft, especially the Me 262 A and the larger Ar 234 B in 1943, became a symbol of advanced technology. They were believed powerful enough to be developed both as close-support bombers against Allied forces on the ground, and as a lethal weapon against the Allies' four-engined bombers and fast fighters. However, only a few small units were established at first, to compile data and introduce new strategies for jet missions. Poor production rates made it impossible to send a sufficient number of Me 262s and Ar 234s to *Luftwaffe* units.

Operational evaluation was initially carried out by *Erprobungskommando* 262 (EK 262 – Trials Unit 262) and *Kommando* Nowotny. EK 262 was established on 19 December 1943 at Lechfeld under the command of *Hauptmann* Thierfelder, but did not receive its first jets until May 1944. Thierfelder died in a Me 262 crash on 18 July 1944. *Hauptmann* Geyer then became the commanding officer of the *Erprobungskommando*, small detachments of which operated from different airfields to gain operational experience. The *Kommando* Nowotny was built up mainly from elements of EK 262 and achieved a number of air victories. It was credited with twenty-two Allied aircraft destroyed, including fast reconnaissance aircraft and Mosquito bombers. Most of the pilots belonging to these units were later sent to *Jagdgeschwader* 7 (JG 7), to train a new generation of pilots to survive jet-propelled missions over the Reich while the Allies enjoyed air superiority.

A first small Me 262 jet bomber formation was already available in late summer 1944. After Willy Messerschmitt had told Adolf Hitler, on several occasions, that his revolutionary Me 262 could carry bombs up to 500 kg, Hitler decided that jet bombers would be able to destroy the advance spearheads of Allied ground forces. However, the limited number of Me 262 A-1a/Bos operated by *Kommando* Schenk (part of *Kampfgeschwader* 51 – KG 51) meant that only local attacks could be carried out over western Europe at that time, to combat the Normandy landings and cover the German retreat from France.

Hitler thought he could win the war on the ground with the help of *'Wunderwaffen'* ('wonder weapons'), and did not heed *General der Jagdflieger* Adolf Galland, who pleaded with him that the Me 262 should be produced solely as a fighter. Hitler insisted that both the Me 262 and the Ar 234 were suitable for use as low-level attack aircraft. But during the early period of jet bombing they were prohibited from flying low-level attacks because the *Luftwaffe* High Command (*Oberkommando der Luftwaffe* – OKL) wanted to prevent high-tech aircraft falling into enemy hands. Furthermore, the 'Identification Friend/Foe' radio equipment, FuG 25, was removed from many German bombers operating over Belgium and the Netherlands, causing German anti-aircraft (AA) batteries close to the front lines to shoot down their own aircraft by mistake.

British and American air raids on the Reich, and several missions flown against key German industries, caused the destruction of many important factories engaged in jet development. In particular, sites all over Bavaria were hit by strongly escorted four-engined bombardment aircraft. The Allies' air superiority in late 1944 and early 1945 made it possible for them to carry out air attacks on German fuel refineries and the transport system. This led to the fuel shortages that would increasingly curtail German air and ground activities. Nevertheless, many Me 262s were produced in dispersed factories and underground production sites near Augsburg, Regensburg and elsewhere, especially in central Germany. Under SS supervision, jet production was increased by an army of slave workers (ie concentration camp inmates). Factories manned by slave labour were the last stronghold of German aircraft production by the end of World War II. However, the loss of important resources and the lack of experienced manpower ensured that the 'wonder weapons' remained but paper dreams.

Operational policy remained entirely defensive because of the lack of new tanks, ammunition and fuel after the *Wehrmacht* retreated from France and Belgium. Until the start of the Ardennes offensive the German High Command (*Oberkommando der Wehrmacht* – OKL) tried to conserve its strength for an effective response to the advancing Allied forces on the north-western German border. The majority of day fighter forces, including II. *Jagdkorps* and 5. *Fliegerdivison*, were transferred from *Luftwaffen-Kommando West* (the command in charge of air operations against the advancing Western Allies) to other parts of Germany. Among those forces remaining in the north-west were the bulk of the jet bombers. Their crews operated at minimum strength over Belgium and the Netherlands, to little effect. Most of Germany's Me 262 fighter units were operated by I. *Jagdkorps*, 2. *Jagddivision* or 7. *Jagddivision*. Their main task was the defence of central Germany and its industries, especially the vital oil targets in the east.

At the end of October 1944 the *Luftwaffen-Kommando West* comprised fewer than twenty-five operational Me 262 bombers and some 620 more fighters, bombers and other military aircraft. For home defence the *Luftflotte Reich* (responsible for internal defence against bombing raids) and all of its subordinated *Luftwaffe* formations could field approximately 900 single-engined fighters, 830 night fighters, and,

lastly, only about ninety jet- and rocket-propelled single-seat aircraft. In addition, some 1000 single-engined fighters were still in operation along the Eastern Front.

During November and December 1944 *Reichsmarschall* Göring ordered the establishment of a massive defence against the Allied bombardment forces, and some more units were transferred to western Germany. Despite the concentration of about 650 fighters, the Allies' overwhelming strength prevented the *Luftwaffe* achieving even limited air superiority, and Allied heavy bombers remained fairly safe from attack. There were too few available Me 262 fighters to have any noticeable effect during the final stage of the air war over the Reich. The same applied to the few Me 262 close-support aircraft operating over western territory now retaken by strong Allied divisions.

By late November the German ground forces had lost major towns in the west, including Metz and Strasbourg. During that desperate time the *Wehrmacht* leadership was planning a big offensive in the Ardennes. The famous German *Panzerdivisions*, supported by as many *Panzergrenadierdivisons* as possible, would attempt to destroy all Allied forces north of the Antwerp–Brussels–Luxembourg line. The *Luftwaffe* command was ordered by Hitler to provide close air support for the ground operations. At that time some thirty Me 262 bombers had been transferred west to forward airfields. This was far too few to achieve more than a very limited success. Although a second Me 262 bomber unit had become operational, the strength of German airpower was broken. But a last offensive was opened early in the morning of 16 December. The *Luftwaffe* supported the ground operations with 2360 aircraft, of which only forty were Ar 234 and Me 262 jet bombers. Most of the aircraft belonging to *Luftwaffen-Kommando West* were single-engined day fighters (1770 of them). Additionally, about 190 day and night ground-attack aircraft (Fw 190s and Ju 87s) were deployed around the German airfields.

Despite gaining some ground in late December, the German forces were pushed back again and could not prevent the Allied advance early in 1945. The devastating Soviet offensive launched in the east in mid-January 1945 also caused the withdrawal of many day fighter formations from the west.

Meanwhile, more Me 262s had been produced and were handed over to front-line *Luftwaffe* units. Between January and February 1945 the Allies kept up the pressure on the Reich. Only occasionally were the Allied spearheads attacked by Me 262 A-1 and A-2 bombers, mainly equipped with fragmentation bombs carried in AB 250 containers. Important bridges which had been captured by the Allies were attacked with larger SD 500 bombs, with mostly limited success. During March 1945 some fifty to sixty operational missions were carried out by German jet bomber forces, with many more being mounted by Fw 190 F fighter-bombers acompanied by the Ju 87 D ground-attack units by dawn or by night.

The number of jet fighters was too low to mount a powerful air attack on a bomber division of the Eighth USAAF over central Germany. But several small attacks carried out by pilots of JG 7 'Nowotny' resulted in German jet pilots claiming some four-engined bombers destroyed. To enlarge the number of jet fighter units within a short period of time the German supreme *Luftwaffen* staff started the reorganisation of their own forces. The II. *Jagdkorps* was disbanded and replaced by both the 14. and the 15. *Fliegerdivision*. The strategic air defence of Germany was similarly reorganised. After the I. *Jagdkorps* was also disbanded, its function was taken over by IX. *Fliegerkorps (Jagd)*, which was to be equipped at first with single-engined day fighters, but then increasingly with fast and powerful Me 262 jets.

The final Russian offensive was aimed at the German capital. By the end of February 1945 the Red Army had reached the general line of the Oder River not far from Berlin. The meagre remaining strength of the German forces was no match for the concentrated enemy attacks. Only a few German jets ever operated against the Eastern Allies, and only shot down a handful of Soviet aircraft.

Attacks on the bridge of Remagen failed despite many desperate low-level raids carried out by *Luftwaffe* pilots flying all kinds of aircraft. Bombs dropped by Me 262s and Ar 234s scored a number of near misses but Allied ground forces continued to cross the Rhine until the bridge collapsed into the river. Further south, some of KG 51's jet bombers were concentrated at the main Frankfurt airfield to fly attacks on the bridgehead in the Oppenheim area.

While these bombing actions were being carried out, Me 262 jet fighters were engaged in attacking four-engined bombers all over central Germany. By April 1945, hopelessly outnumbered and suffering from fuel shortages, only a limited number of Me 262s of JG 7 could continue the home defence. At this time, the forces operated by JG 7 were supported by the first *Kampfgeschwader (Jagd)*, the KG (J) 54. But the unit was severely hit by many Allied air raids during its working up. Furthermore, it lost many poorly trained fighter (ex-bomber) pilots in action due their lack of operational experience of fighter tactics, most having previously piloted medium bombers, such as the He 111 or the Ju 88 A-4.

Other *Kampfgeschwader (Jagd)* units were established early in 1945, but there were not enough Me 262 A-1a fighters to supply more than a few jets to these formations. Therefore most of the new KG (J)s received Bf 109 G-6, G-10 and G-14 aircraft instead to carry out day fighter operations until more Me 262s could be produced. Only a few Me 262 jets were handed over to KG (6). Parts of III. *Gruppe* became operational in April 1945. KG (J) 30 had started jet training early in 1945, but possibly never flew missions in action.

Despite the output of Me 262s and of the Ar 234 bombers, the Allied forces were never opposed by strong formations of either German jet type. The operational roles, the air-to-air combat and low-level attacks split the weak forces of the *Luftwaffe* once more. Hitler's early obsession with close-support action hindered a more successful air strategy, as did Göring's failure to support Adolf Galland's requests for a large-scale concentrated piston-fighter attack against one of the Eighth USAAF raids and for the employment of the Me 262 solely as a defensive fighter aircraft. Late in the war Hitler changed his mind and ordered as many jet fighters as possible to be built. Germany's war power had been virtually destroyed, but the last resources were thrown into the battle.

However, early in 1945, *Reichsminister* Speer issued a secret report which forecast the ultimate defeat of German power in April 1945 without Allied forces having to occupy the remaining territory held by the *Wehrmacht*.

The first very clear signs of the dissolution and disintegration of the German *Luftwaffe* forces in the remaining war theatres were seen early in April 1945. The further course of the war split German forces into a southern and a northern region. More and more *Luftwaffe* airfields were being overrun. Retreating supply units were overtaken by enemy ground forces. On 26 April, the Western and Eastern Allies met near Torgau on the Elbe.

Meanwhile, two new *Luftwaffe* formations had entered the jet war. In the north the first *Staffeln* of *Jagdgeschwader* 1 (JG 1) had handed over their Fw 190 As to other units and received their first He 162, the *'Volksjäger'* ('people's fighter'). The lack of jet fuel (J2) meant that this single-engined jet fighter could only be used for a very few missions against RAF intruder and low-level attack aircraft. The surviving parts of JG 1 surrendered during the last days of May 1945. Most *'Volksjäger'* were handed over to the RAF authorities.

General Adolf Galland had meanwhile taken over the command of JV 44 (*'Jagdverband'* – 'fighter formation' – because it was not a standard *'Jagdgeschwader'* – 'fighter unit'), and gave many pilots the opportunity to fly a superior jet aircraft during the last days of a lost war. His unit operated – as did many others – from the *Reichsautobahn* near Munich, and was quickly withdrawn to Salzburg airport in May 1945. Before American ground forces overran the unit's new airfield some Me 262s had been evacuated to meadows near Innsbruck, and later became war booty. The order sent to JV 44 to join JG 7 as a fourth jet fighter *Gruppe* and to move to Prague-Rusin was never carried out.

The last, weak German jet formations were concentrated around Prague. These forces comprised parts of JG 7, KG (J) 6 and KG 51. Late in April 1945 the jet pilots carried out low-level attacks against Russian ground forces in central Germany but suffered many losses due to a high concentration of AA units operated by the Red Army. Late in April 1945 the *Gefechtsver-* band ('battle unit') Hogeback (operating the remaining aircraft of KG (J) 6, minor parts of I. and II./KG (J) 54 and the KG 51) was ordered to support German ground forces after Czechoslovakian resistance fighters had attacked all German-held positions in the Prague area. After the final ground attack sorties had been carried out early in May 1945, the last jet planes took part in a final mission. Then the pilots flew to British-held positions in northern Germany near Fassberg.

Apart from the units already mentioned, a number of others had been established by the OKL. Besides the *Ergänzungsjagdgeschwader* 2, a training unit for jet pilots, the III. (*Ergänzungsgruppe*)/*Kampfgeschwader* was set up in order to train more jet fighter-bomber pilots. In addition, some more experimental units flew the Me 262 or other German jets. For example, the *Kommando* Stamp tested the bombardment of Allied bomber formations with the help of small fragmentation bombs or larger GP bombs towards the end of 1944. The results were poor, and so the pilots and aircraft were given to other units.

The 1./*Versuchsverband* of OKL started experiments to carry out short-range reconnaissance missions. Later on, the *Nahaufklärungsgruppe* 6 was established in Herzogenaurach in November 1944. One of its two *Staffeln* was commanded by *Hauptmann* Braunegg, the commanding officer who operated the *Kommando* Braunegg from the Münster area early in 1945. The establishment of other short-range units was ordered early in 1945, but these units saw only limited operational deployment.

These formations and all of the fighter and jet bomber units were dissolved during the last days of World War II. The operational experience of the personnel was not lost, despite the War's disastrous end for Germany, as it was taken over by the Allies and used for combat training by all the victorious nations. Most of the jet aircraft still airworthy were sent to France, Great Britain and the USA. Many paper projects and jet engines were also captured by advancing Allied ground formations. These war prizes formed the basis for the construction of more powerful jet aircraft in the following years.

The new Me 262 V7 (WerkNr. 170303), which joined the Messerschmitt flight evaluation on 19 October 1944. This was the prototype for the rebuilt conversion Me 262 A-1a/Bo. The aircraft was tested at *Lager* Lechfeld with 1000 kp take-off assistance rockets and different heavy military loads. Two rocket propulsion units can be seen (left) under the camouflage netting.

Above: Another Me 262 A awaits trials at *Lager* Lechfeld, where most of the Me 262 test programme was carried out. The flight test programme was worked out in close co-operation with the *Kommando der Erprobungsstellen* (KdE) at Rechlin, the *Oberkommando der Luftwaffe* (OKL) and the aircraft producer to save time. In the meantime the development of the Ar 234, Ju 388 and a few other aircraft was also being undertaken at Rechlin.

Below: One practice GP bomb, in the size of a SC 500 but without explosive load and fuse, is prepared for loading action by employees of the Messerschmitt works at *Lager* Lechfeld. The air base was bombed several times by Allied bombers, and most of the buildings were severely hit, but this did not stop the work on the new generation of jet fighters.

Right: A view into the cockpit of a Me 262 A-1a single-seat day fighter which was captured by American forces at *Lager* Lechfeld in April 1945. On the left side of the panel are the flight instruments, and on the right side are two rows of instruments to monitor both Jumo 004 B turbo-jets. The engine controls were installed on the left console, the electric systems on the right.

Left: After a flight with a performance of more than 1000 km/h the Messerschmitt factory pilot Heinz Herlitzius enjoys a cigarette. Together with Herlitzius, Dr Hermann Wurster, Fritz Wendel, Wilhelm Ostertag and many other experienced flyers succeeded in completing the ambitious test programme in a remarkable period of time, considering the handicaps imposed by wartime conditions.

Early in 1945 two Me 262 A-1as of III. *Gruppe* of *Ergänzungsjagdgeschwader* 2 (III./EJG 2), 'White 6' and 'White 13', take off to intercept bombers of the Fifteenth USAF approaching the area of Munich–Augsburg–Landsberg. As well as training new jet pilots, the instructors, under the command of *Oberstleutnant* Heinz Bär, also flew operations against enemy planes over Bavaria.

Above: This fin section, fitted with woollen tufts, was tested at *Lager* Lechfeld. As well as the prototype Me 262 V2 (WerkNr. 170056), which was tested there to check improved side rudders, eight other re-designated prototypes were also used for different evaluations. These included the new Me 262 V1 with various wooden tail surfaces, and both Me 262 A-2a/U2 two-seat bombers.

Below: A close-up view of the Jumo 004 B turbo-jet engine of a Me 262 A-1a. The first Jumo 004s were installed under the wings of a Me 262 prototype, the V4, which took off for the first time with two Jumo 004 A-0s on 15 May 1943. On 17 October 1943 the Me 262 V6 took off with the help of two improved Jumo 004 B-0s. After first series Jumo 004 B-1s had arrived at *Lager* Lechfeld, trials were carried out with the Me 262 V8 on 18 March 1944.

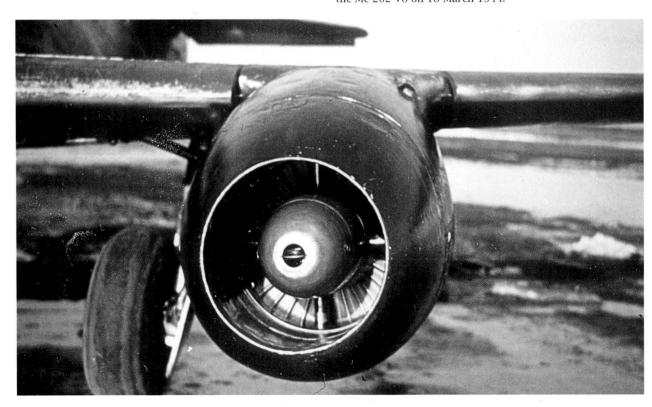

The night fighter prototype Me 262 V2 (WerkNr. 170056) was tested with FuG 216 and FuG 218 radar installations and a complete weapons bay to evaluate the influence of the fire power resulting from four 30 mm machine cannon. There is no proof that this prototype was ever used in combat action against British night bombers or fighters.

The fin and rudder of a He 162 single-seat day fighter captured by British forces at Leck in northern Germany and later hand-ed over, together with a few more 'Volksjäger', to the French Allies. The Allies had their own jet-propelled designs, and used the He 162s solely to examine Germany's military jet aircraft technology.

Above: The He 280 prototype jet fighter, which joined flight development on 22 September 1940, and crashed, after sixty-four towed flights, on 13 January 1943. The He 280 V1 had no tendency to flutter and attained a maximum speed of 800 km/h. The installation of four Argus As 014 units under the He 280's wings was later proposed.

Right: Under the leadership of Mach and Regner, this mock-up and one other had been constructed by June 1939. As of July 1939 more studies were carried out featuring a twin-engined jet aircraft with a nose wheel. At that time the future He 280 was still designated He 180. By late summer 1940 numerous details had been resolved and Heinkel offered the hitherto private project to the *Reichsluftfahrtministerium* (RLM).

Left: The third prototype, with the registration GJ+CB, which joined the evaluation phase on 30 March 1941. It was propelled by two Heinkel He S8A jet engines, but these did not perform well and were replaced by more powerful Jumo 004 jets. On 26 June 1943 the aircraft was very badly damaged on a test flight, due to the failure of one engine.

Opposite page, bottom: During the weapons adjustment the forward section of the He 280's fuselage was fixed on a movable trestle in order to check the behaviour of all three MG 151 machine guns being installed in the nose. Several attempts had to be carried out before a sufficient ammunition supply was finally achieved.

Below: The He 280 V3, towed by an old tractor and accompanied by several maintenance personnel. The He 280 V3 (GJ+CB) was first flown on 5 July 1942. At the end of World War II parts of the prototype were captured at Schwechat near Vienna.

Above: As well as the He 280 V1 to V3, two other He 280 aircraft were assembled. The He 280 V7 (D-IEXM, NU+EB), seen here, and the He 280 V8 (NU+EC), joined flight testing by April and July 1943 respectively. The seventh He 280 had made 115 towed flights by early 1945. The He 280 V8 was also tested with a V-tail unit with the help of the *Deutsche Forschungsanstalt für Segelflug* (DFS) near Vienna.

Left: The experimental department of the Messerschmitt works in Augsburg-Haunstetten. Behind a Bf 108 (TJ+AY) liaison aircraft is the first prototype Me 262 powered by a Jumo 210 G piston engine (production number – WerkNr. – 42 012). A Caudron C 445 belonging to the factory is in the background. On 4 August 1941 the Me 262 V1 prototype (PC+UA, WerkNr. 262 00 001) was flown by two pilots, Bader and Beauvais, from Rechlin.

Above: The second prototype Me 262 jet aircraft, which had the registration PC+UB (WerkNr. 262 00 002). The aircraft was still named 'P 1065', although it received its official number 262 by February 1941. The aircraft, which was fitted with two Jumo 109-004 turbo-jets, crashed on 18 April 1943, killing factory test pilot Ostertag.

Below: The third prototype Me 262, which was completed early in 1942. The lack of turbo-jets kept it at the factory while production of the Me 262 V4 and V5 continued. On 18 July 1942 the first jet-powered take-off was made, by Fritz Wendel at Leipheim air base. The factory pilot returned to Leipheim with no difficulty some ten minutes later. In the background of this picture a Me 321 transport glider can be seen.

Above: Another view of the third prototype Me 262, placed before one of the huge Me 321 gliders being built at Leipheim near the *Reichsautobahn* leading to Munich. The third Me 262 was damaged on 11 August 1942 during take-off on its seventh flight, with Dipl.-Ing. Heinrich Beauvais at the controls. The engines overheated and neither delivered the necessary thrust for take-off. The aircraft was repaired and flew again on 5 March 1943.

Below: *Reichsmarschall* Hermann Göring (in light uniform, left) visiting *Lager* Lechfeld near Landsberg/Bavaria on 2 November 1943, accompanied by Willy Messerschmitt and *General* Adolf

Galland. The evaluation of the Me 262 continued at this air base until April 1945, with only minor interruptions despite several Allied air raids.

Opposite page: A detail of the forward landing gear of the Me 262 V6 (VI+AA, WerkNr. 130001), which could be fully retracted by a hydraulic system. This picture was taken at Augsburg-Haunstetten. In the background, artificial trees camouflage the factory airport. The V6 was first flown on 17 October 1943 and crashed after twenty-eight test flights during a further test by Kurt Schmidt on 8 March 1944.

Left: Gerd Lindner brings his flight demonstration of the grey-painted Me 262 V6 to an end, observed by a group of *Luftwaffe* officers inspecting the factory site at *Lager* Lechfeld. Göring and many officers sent by the RLM were reportedly amazed by the performance and manoeuvrability of the twin-engined jet plane, which was fitted with two Jumo 004 B-0 turbo-jets.

Below: The Me 262 S3 (VI+AH, WerkNr. 130008), which was first flown on 16 April 1944. It was the third pre-production series aircraft and differed not much from the later Me 262 A-1b aircraft, which was also fitted with four heavy MK 108 machine cannon. The Me 262 S3 was handed over to *Erprobungs-kommando* 262 (EK 262) and was damaged after shedding a turbo-jet following a nose-gear collapse.

Above: The sixth Me 262, called S6 (VI+AK, WerkNr. 130011), which was first flown in April 1944 and crashed on 18 July 1944. The aircraft was given to EK 262, an experimental fighter unit formed at *Lager* Lechfeld on 19 December 1943. Its first commander was *Hauptmann* Werner Thierfelder who was killed on 18 July 1944 and was replaced by *Hauptmann* Horst Geyer in August 1944.

Below: A few Me 262 fighters and bombers were evaluated not at *Lager* Lechfeld but at Rechlin near Lake Müritz near Neustrelitz. In the latter war years almost all evaluation took place at *Lager* Lechfeld, and in early 1945 only one Me 262 (WerkNr. 111609) was operated by the *Kommando der Erprobungsstellen* (KdE) at the Rechlin *Luftwaffe* base. The aircraft was used to compile performance data.

Left: Herr Lüttgau, the main factory photographer, took this photograph during the flight evaluation of the third prototype Me 262. Many additional installations increased the flight weight of the early prototypes too much and resulted in the development of larger retractable landing gears.

Opposite page, bottom: *Oberstleutnant* Heinz Bär, the commanding officer of III. *Gruppe* of *Ergänzungsjagdgeschwader* 2 (III./EJG 2) based at Lechfeld, flew the 'Red 13' several times to intercept Allied war planes over southern Germany. He invariably numbered his machines (from Bf 109 and

Fw 190 to Me 262) '13' for good luck. Bär shot down his last P-47 on 28 April 1945. He claimed a total of 220 air victories and completed over 1000 missions.

Below: Heinz Bär sitting on the wing of his famous jet fighter. He made his first jet flight in September 1944 at Wenzendorf near Hamburg. Then he took over the command of III./EJG 2 and additionally tested rocket-armed Me 262s and also wing bombs and other new weaponry. His first air victory flying a Me 262 A-1a was on 19 March 1945 when he succeeded in destroying a P-51 fighter.

Below: Another view of *Oberstleutnant* Bär's Me 262 at *Lager* Lechfeld. By the time he took over the command of *Jagdverband* 44 after *General* Galland was wounded in action, he had shot down, in the Me 262, one P-51, three P-47s, two B-26s and two B-24s. As commander of JV 44 he claimed his next B-26, two P-47s and two P-51s over Bavaria. Heinz Bär died after the war, when his light plane crashed near Brunswick, on 28 April 1957.

Bottom: A Me 262 A-1a of *Jagdverband* 44. JV 44 existed from 24 February 1945 to 1 May 1945. Commanded by *Generalleutnant* Adolf Galland, the former *General der Jagdflieger* (GdJ), it had a provisional strength of sixteen Me 262 A-1a fighter aircraft. The ground personnel was taken from 16./JG 54, *Industrieschutzstaffel* 1 (Industrial Defence Squadron 1) and from III./EJG 2. After operating from the Munich region the JV 44 moved to Salzburg for its final missions.

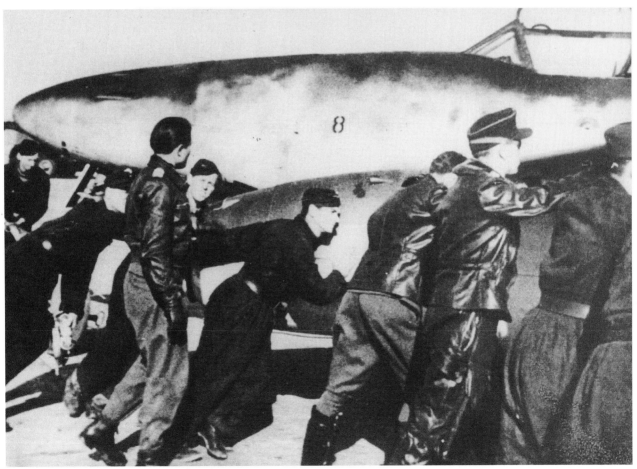

Above: The junk yard at Prague after the end of World War II. Most of the Me 262 fragments seen in the foreground would formerly have belonged to aircraft operated by the *Gefechtsverband* ('battle unit') Hogeback, which was responsible for attacking enemy positions around the Czech capital early in May 1945. As long as supplies lasted, the strongholds were bombed with small fragmentation SD 1s. Several low-level attacks were also flown.

Below: During the Allied advance through Bavaria there were a lot of displaced Me 262 A-1a jets captured along the roads. This one was found near Leipheim before taking off from the local *Reichsautobahn*.

Above: A jet at the Neuburg air base belonging to *Kampfgeschwader (Jagd)* 54, a former bomber unit which had to change its operational role at the end of 1944. Enemy action also forced KG (J) 54, which consisted of three *Gruppen*, to change its bases. Flying from Gardelegen, Kitzingen, Neuburg and Munich-Riem, the unit suffered many losses to Allied P-51 and P-47 piston fighters during take-off and landing.

Opposite page, top: This Me 262 A-1a was operated from Neuburg by KG (J) 54. The air base was hit by fragmentation bombs during many Allied air raids, and several Messerschmitt jets were damaged. This one stood at Neuburg until summer 1945, waiting to be scrapped.

Right: These jets belonged to KG (J) 54, commanded by *Oberstleutnant* Volprecht Riedesel *Freiherr* zu Eisenbach. On 9 February 1945 he and many others were killed in action against American bombers. *Major* Hans-Georg Bättcher became the new commanding officer on 27 February 1945. Enemy action forced his *Geschwaderstab* to move from Giebelstadt to Zerbst and Fürstenfeldbruck. It was finally disbanded at Holzkirchen in Bavaria.

Opposite page, top: To avoid destruction during Allied raids, many Me 262 were dismantled and put beside the air bases all over the Reich in order to replace the casualties occurring on the ground or in the air. The aircraft shown had been part of the KG (J) 54 and were formerly operated by the 2. *Staffel* at Prague.

Left: Together with five to ten instructors, *Oberstleutnant* Bär carried out final attacks over Bavaria at the end of World War II, flying the Me 262 A-1a series as shown. He was said to be one of the few pilots to fly the rocket-assisted Me 262 C-1 conversion.

Above: The 'Green 1' was operated by staff of III. *Gruppe* of *Jagdgeschwader* 7 'Nowotny' (III./JG 7), which was based at Parchim in March 1945. There, a few Me 262 had been tested with rocket launchers fitted under the forward part of the fuselage. Note the small trolley (left) delivering more rockets to the aircraft. Many more Me 262 A-1as were equipped with R4M-missiles fixed under the wings.

Above: The huge tent behind the Me 262 A-1a had formerly belonged to a circus. After British and American bombers of the Eighth and Fifteenth Air Force had damaged the *Luftwaffe* infrastructure early in 1945, provisional shelters like this were utilised, but it became impossible to maintain and service the remaining Me 262 jets in central Germany and Bavaria.

Below: During the final weeks of World War II the improved airport of Munich-Riem, together with Erding and Fürsten-feldbruck, became the home of German jets. The taxiing Me 262 A-1a is here returning to Riem from an interception mission over Bavaria in April 1945.

Opposite page, top: Hermann Göring, accompanied by Adolf Galland (left), visited units in Bavaria which were chosen to become a part of German jet fighter forces. The first Me 262 units were set up from the III. *Gruppe* of the *Zerstörergeschwader* 26, whose pilots were familiar with twin-engined aircraft (Bf 110s and Me 410s). This was considered an advantage when converting to the Me 252 twin jet.

Opposite page, bottom: Rear view of a Me 262 fighter-bomber with two bomb racks. Orders were issued late in 1943 for the development of fast jet-propelled aircraft other than the Me 262 fighters. On 12 December 1943 Adolf Hitler had called for commitment of the Me 262 as a single-seat fighter-bomber to counter the long-awaited invasion of the Allies in western Europe. On 8 June 1944 the Führer restricted the further development of day fighter versions of the Me 262, as he intended it to be used as a retaliatory bomber.

Above: In July 1944 the delivery of the new jet-propelled fighter-bombers like this one began. Under the designation 'Stormbird', the first ones were delivered to *Kommando* Schenk, which was ordered to launch bombing raids with only a few Me 262 As fitted with ETC pylons to carry SC 250 bombs or AB 250 bomb containers. The Allied forces had won a large bridgehead along the Normandy coast and concentrated a lot of AA forces to protect their own positions against Me 262s.

Opposite page, top: A Me 262 A-1a/Bo carrying a SC 250 general purpose bomb on ETCs commonly called *'Wikingerschiffe'* ('viking ships'). Bombing raids had little effect at this point, because Adolf Hitler prohibited low-level raids behind the front lines in western Europe, and from an altitude of several thousand feet there was no chance of hitting important individual targets such as bridges.

Right: A close view of a Me 262 A-1a/Bo with two SC 250 bombs hanging beneath the forward fuselage. In order to reduce weight two of the MK 108s have been removed. The openings were later faired over to reduce air drag. German resources had diminished to the extent that only a limited number of jets were converted into fighter bombers. The planned definitive series, called A-2a, was also built only in limited numbers.

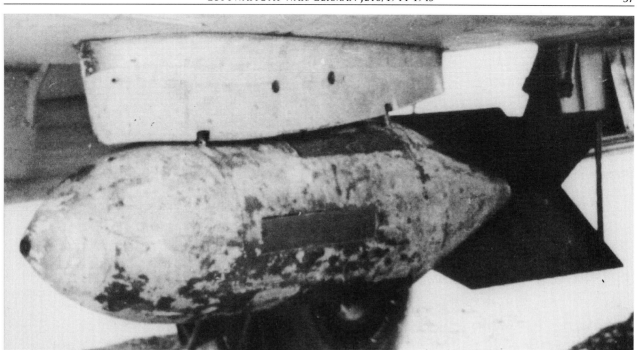

Above: This photograph was taken in Bavaria late in 1944 during the evaluation of the Me 262 jet bomber. Trials were undertaken to service the jets outside well equipped bases, with a minimum of *matériel* and special equipment. The small starter trolley was needed to charge the batteries of this Me 262 A-1a/Bo and to enable the ignition of both Jumo 004 turbo-jets.

Below: On 5 December 1944 *Major* Wolfgang Schenk, the former operational leader of '*Sonderkommando Edelweiss*' who had tested Me 262 fighter-bombers like this one, became the new commanding officer of *Kampfgeschwader* 51. During winter 1944/45 the operations of KG 51 were limited by many factors, including weather conditions and the lack of fuel and spare parts. From Rheine and Hopsten the Me 262 A-1 and A-2 jet bombers had to attack Allied positions all over Belgium and the Netherlands.

Above: The Me 262s were maintained under poor conditions before being involved in operations when the German offensive in the Ardennes began on 16 December 1944. Six days later Me 262 pilots of KG 51 started their attacks against Allied supply lines leading to the battlefields in the Ardennes. In mid-December 1944 the preparations for 'Unternehmen BODENPLATTE' entered an important phase. On 1 January 1945 some of these aircraft took off to attack targets in the Brussels and Arnhem–Eindhoven area.

Below: Several low-level attacks were carried out after Hitler finally gave permission for them. In the meantime some parts of KG 51 had been moved back to Giebelstadt and Frankfurt, to mount bomb attacks against targets in Alsace where French units moved forward to the Rhine and threatened southern Germany.

Above: One of the rare Me 262 A-2a/U2 two-seat high-speed jet bombers, and a second Me 262 aircraft behind it, are towed into position by an Opel 'Blitz'. Note the (partially covered) new glazed nose designed to accommodate a prone bomb aimer. Only two prototypes of this aircraft were constructed, and they never saw any operational usage with the *Luftwaffe*. During a test flight, one of them, designated Me 262 V 555, crashed near Marburg and was later captured by American ground forces.

Below: The abandoned 'White 14' early in 1945 after being captured by American troops. A training aircraft, this was possibly operated first by *Kommando* Nowotny, then by JG 7 and finally by III./EJG 2. Structural defects finally prevented any further operational missions.

Opposite page, bottom: Selected high-ranking NSDAP leaders in autumn 1944 were invited to visit a *Luftwaffe* base to see the new '*Wunderwaffen*' that would supposedly win the War. The aircraft shown here is coded E2+02. It was part of the inventory of the *Erprobungsstelle* Rechlin near Lake Müritz in central eastern Germany.

Above: Me 262 aircraft marked with a small or large 'S' (seen here within the fuselage cross) could only be used for training missions. Several of these were former operational aircraft which had been damaged. Such aircraft were handed over either to III./EJG 2 or to the *Ergänzungskampfgeschwader* which was responsible for training jet bomber pilots at the end of World War II.

Above: A small number of two-seater Me 262 training aircraft like this one were produced by Blohm & Voss at Wenzendorf near Hamburg after it became clear that the *Deutsche Lufthansa* at Staaken could not fulfil the task. First a pre-series aircraft (WerkNr. 130010) was built, followed by other B-1s rebuilt from A-1s despite a severe air raid in January 1945.

Below: The production of Me 262 aircraft continued in 1945, despite severe Allied air raids. The former production sites were split up into several smaller ones which were dispersed around Stuttgart, Ulm, Augsburg, Munich and Regensburg. One of these, shown here, was the '*Waldfabrik* Obertraubling' ('Obertraubling forest factory') east of Regensburg, where the final assembly took place.

Opposite page, top: At Obertraubling Me 262 A-1a fighters were produced in a well-camouflaged woodland assembly site called 'forest assembly', which was finally captured by American ground troops late in April 1945. In the course of the War some 1430 Me 262s were built, of which more than 800 reached the *Luftwaffe*'s front line units.

Right: The first stage of this huge construction, near Landsberg on Lech, was finished early in 1945. Two huge bunkers, called 'Weingut I' and 'Weingut II' were planned, for the production of greater than ever numbers of Me 262s, under safe conditions and a thick layer of concrete. Slave labour was used in a bid to finish the work, but the Allies ended all such attempts in April 1945. The completed parts were later used as supply stores by the new, post-war German Air Force.

Above: The right combustion chamber of the composite engine explodes during testing of the sole Me 262 C-2b interceptor at Lechfeld on 25 February 1945. The first flight of the C-2b took place on 26 March 1945. Climbing at a speed of 120 m/s the home defence aircraft reached an altitude of 8200 m in not more than 1½ minutes.

Below: American specialists checked the remains of the Lechfeld testing site at the end of April 1945. Besides several other Me 262 prototype and series aircraft, the former Me 262 V074 (WerkNr. 170074) was captured. Its engines had been removed. Additional material was found describing a third

home defence aircraft, 'C-3a', a Me 262 A-1 fitted with a jettisonable rocket engine and two 600-litre drop tanks.

Right: The Me 262 V083 was captured at Lechfeld in April 1945. This and another jet fighter were designed as *'Pülkzerstörer'* ('pack destroyers'), equipped with a huge 50 mm Mauser cannon in the nose designed to attack and break up 'boxes' of American bombers. By 21 March 1945 the first of these prototypes had made nineteen flights. When a second aircraft became available, *Major* Wilhelm Herget did in fact attack a pack of B-26 bombers, on 16 April 1945.

Below: The first photo-reconnaissance unit equipped with Me 262 A-1a/U3 aircraft, like the one shown here, was set up in November 1943 at Herzogen-aurach near Nuremburg. It was decided to form a *Gruppen*-staff together with two *Staffeln* under the command of *Major* Heinz Schütze. A small evaluation unit, *Kommando* Braunegg, was also established to gain operational knowledge for future combat action over western Europe.

Opposite page, top: In February 1945 the *Kommando* Braunegg, operating under the command of *Oberleutnant* (later *Hauptmann*) Herward Braunegg, saw combat action over north-west Germany subordinated under the command of *Versuchsverband* OKL. The *Kommando* was integrated with its few Me 262 A-1as and Me 262 A-1a/U3s into the short-range reconnaissance unit 2. *Nahauf- klärungsgruppe* 6 (2./NAG 6).

Opposite page, bottom: The NAG 6 operated from Kaltenkirchen near Hamburg, Hohne in Schleswig, Burg near Magdeburg, and Fassberg. The unit was then forced to retreat to Bavaria, where the first reconnaissance Me 262s of 2./NAG 6, like this one, landed on 13 April 1945 at Lechfeld, where staff and the first *Staffel* had been stationed since 27 March 1945. The last missions were flown in April 1945.

Above: This Me 262 A-1a/U1 possibly belonged to 1./NAG 1, the second short-range reconnaissance unit. A few Me 262 A-1a/U1s were delivered to the unit in March 1945 and flew a limited number of operational missions from Zerbst in central Germany. Only about thirty aircraft were handed over to 1./NAG 1, NAG 6 and 3./NAG 13 in the closing days of the War.

Below: To secure the close defence of the Me 262 key production sites some small *Industrieschutzstaffeln* (ISS) – Industrial Defence Squadrons – were raised. The first was established in late 1944. One of them was based at *Lager* Lechfeld, shown here. The aircraft were flown by factory pilots from the local Messerschmitt works.

Above: Aircraft outside one of the huge hangars at the Erding air base. The Allied forces found the Me 262s gathered before one of these severely damaged hangars in May 1945. Several *Luftwaffe* aircraft were made operational at Erding. The *'Frontschleuse'* (Forward Air Depot) there was responsible for installing the weapons and the wireless operation systems. Another task was rebuilding operational aircraft.

Below: The shattered remains of the *Luftwaffe* filled many air bases. Only a few Me 262s could be taken to America for further evaluation.

Right: A old wooden mock-up of the Ar 234 B-2 twin-engined jet bomber, with the cockpit roof removed to reveal the interior to visiting officers sent by RLM and the *Kommando der Erprobungs-stellen* (KdE), the main evaluation unit of the *Luftwaffe*.

Above: The closed structure included a periscope in the roof, to look for enemy fighters attacking from the rear. Two heavy fixed guns fitted in the rear fuselage were intended to protect fast bombers during their missions. In the middle of the cockpit was the bomb sight. The engine's instruments were installed on the right console.

Opposite page, top: A close-up of the wooden mock-up on which many modifications and installations were checked for later usage. On the left side are the throttle levers. All the flight instruments

were on a console in the pilot's view. In front of the bomber pilot is the periscope eyepiece, and beyond his feet the bomb sight. Mock-ups like this were used for Ar 234 B and C conversions.

Opposite page, bottom: A view of the wooden fuselage of the actual size mock-up of the Berta version of the Ar 234. Bomb loads could be tested under the mid-fuselage section, using wooden dummies. Trials were later carried out with real bombs, without their explosive load and fuses. It was possible to load armour piercing bombs up to 1000 kg.

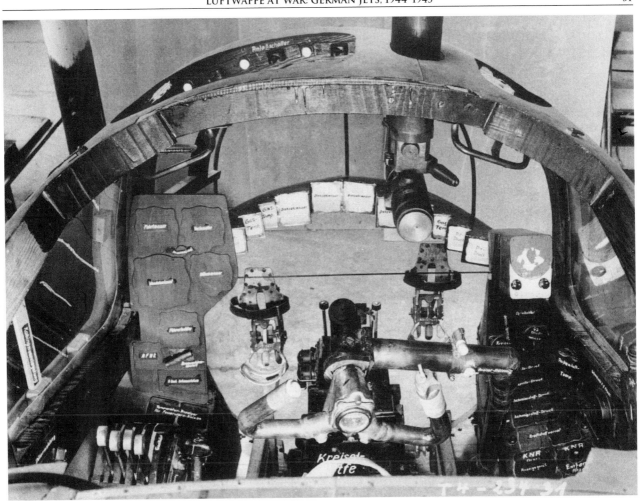

Above: Jettisonable rocket sets greatly aided taking off with heavy bomb loads. At smaller bases these packs assumed an added significance because Allied bomb raids caused the demolition of the main runways. In order to secure a limited operational action over western Europe it was necessary for all forward air fields to have rocket sets in stock.

Below: The ground crew of III./KG 76 carries a 1000 kg GP bomb to one of the Ar 234 Bs hidden in a forest near Rheine. Loads like this were often towed with the help of a *Kettenkrad* (tracked motorcycle combination). The bomber in the background is already loaded for its next action over the front.

Above: An Opel 'Blitz' lorry, used also as a refuelling vehicle, here tows an Ar 234 B photo-reconnaissance aircraft to the runway. Among the first experienced reconnaissance pilots were Horst Götz, Erich Sommer and Werner Muffey. *Oberleutnant* Muffey flew with the *Kommando* Sperling. His Ar 234 B had the designation T9+KH. It was often fitted with two drop tanks to enlarge its operational range in combat.

Below: Refuelling one of the Ar 234s of *Kommando* Sperling from an Opel truck. These reconnaissance jets became the sole source of up-to-date information about Allied supply lines behind the front. They were also called upon to watch British harbours and monitor hits by the German *Vergeltungswaffen*, the V1s and V2s, all over southern England, and especially in the London area.

Left and above: Two views of the wooden mock-up of the camera installations inside the rear section of the Ar 234's fuselage. These photographs may have belonged to a series of prints sent to the RLM before a first prototype jet reconnaissance aircraft was rebuilt from the Ar 234 V5 (taking off with the aid of a pair of jettisonable wheels, and landing on a sprung skid attachment). A *'Rüstsatz'* (conversion kit) later became available, comprising two cameras (Rb 50/30 or 75/30).

Above: An Ar 234 B of the first *Staffel* of *Fernaufklärungsgruppe* 123. This was one of the few jet reconnaissance aircraft that took part in the last retreating action from northern Germany and Denmark to Norway. On 1 May 1945 it was flown from Rendsburg near Kiel to Stavanger, where it was captured by British and Norwegian forces shortly after.

Below: One of the late Ar 234 C prototypes – the V21 – powered by four BMW 003 A-1 turbo-jets. This aircraft (WerkNr. 130061, PI+WZ) first took off on 24 November 1944 and was still in action in February 1945. It was mainly used for testing the flight behaviour and performance of the four-engined conversion, until 18 February 1945.

Above and below: The exterior of the wooden mock-up of the projected Ar 234 C-5, which differed from the series C-3 cabin in many ways. The main instrument board was now located in front of the pilot. The C-5 was a two-seat bomber whose second crew member could perform the duties of a wireless operator, navigator and bomb aimer. This enabled the pilot to concentrate on his own task, flying the bomber to the assigned target.

Opposite page: Two further views into the cockpit of an Ar 234 bomber mock-up. In order to improve the abilities of the two- and four-engined bombers, ever more modern instruments were installed, such as the FuG 101, a very exact altimeter for precise low-level attacks. A rear warning system, improved bomb sight and fixed forward firing armament were also proposed.

Right and below: Constant attempts were made to improve the range of vision of a second crew member, sitting not far behind the pilot in the Ar 234 C's cockpit. The radar installation is near the bulge for the observer, who would enter his compartment from steps at the side of the forward fuselage while the pilot took his seat from the other side of the cabin. This arrangement differed not much from the night fighters of the proposed P-series.

Above: The damaged Ar 234 prototype, which was hit during the American air raid at Wesendorf on 4 April 1945. The aircraft belonged to a new series of prototypes equipped with four BMW 003 engines. The Ar 234 V20 was first flown on 5 November 1944 with Ubbo Janssen at the controls. On 28 March 1945 it was transferred to Warnemünde and then Wesendorf.

Opposite page, top: This badly damaged Ar 234 C crashed near Bad Wörishofen, probably in late April 1945. It is believed that this was one of the C aircraft flown to Bavaria to prevent them falling

into the hands of Allied forces in northern Germany. Others landed at Munich-Riem, and were captured a few days later.

Opposite page, bottom: The Ju 287 V1 was the first prototype of a German heavy jet bomber. The lack of more powerful turbo-jets forced Junkers to install four Jumo 004 engines. The prototype was rebuilt from the fuselage of an He 177 and utilised parts from many other aircraft. The landing gear of an American B-24 heavy bomber was used to enable it to begin flight evaluation as quickly as possible.

Above: A front view of the first Ju 287 prototype. It was flown for the first time on 8 August 1944, propelled by four Jumo 004 B engines and three rocket engines called *'Krafteier'* (literally 'power eggs') fixed under the wing nacelles and one of the forward turbo-jet engines. This huge jet bomber had a top speed of 370 km/h. The Ju 287 V1 was flown by *Flugkapitän* Siegfried Holzbauer.

Left: Two Ju 287 prototypes were destroyed by German soldiers at Brandis air base. The aircraft in this picture was the second prototype, equipped with double engine nacelles under both wings and single turbo-jets side by side on the forward fuselage. In September 1944 it was ordered that all Jumo 004 B jet engines should be removed and brought to Rechlin, to provide propulsion for Me 262 aircraft being evaluated. In February 1945 both Ju 287 prototypes were blown up.

Below: The unpowered Horten H IX V1 was towed to its start position by a heavy truck before its first flight over Göttingen. On 5 March 1944 the prototype was towed by a He 111 up to an altitude of some 4000 m. It was later transported for testing at Oranienburg on 23 March 1944.

Bottom: The H IX V2 taking shape in a hangar at Göttingen in November 1944. The aircraft was fitted with two Jumo 004 B turbojets. The first take-off was on 18 December 1944 at Oranienburg with Erwin Ziller at the controls. A few months later the aircraft was captured by advancing American soldiers at Brandis near Leipzig.

Above: The second H IX was flown for the first time by test-pilot *Leutnant* Erwin Ziller at Oranienburg air base near the German capital. On 2 February 1945 one of the two Jumo 004 B engines failed. During the emergency landing the H IX V2 crashed, killing Ziller.

Below: There were further proposals to build as many of the improved *Göttinger Ausführung* ('Göttingen Variant') as possible. Now built by the Gothaer Waggonfabrik, it was known as the Go 229 A-1. The third prototype was captured before flying and was brought to the USA after Germany's unconditional surrender in May 1945. The Go 229 V5 shown here was under construction at Friedrichsroda near Gotha and was scrapped in 1945.

Opposite page, top: The early He 162s, like this one, were constructed by Heinkel Süd in the Vienna region in October 1944. The first of these, the He 162 V1 (WerkNr. 200001, VI+IA), had its maiden flight on 6 December 1944. It was followed by more than twenty prototypes until a first series He 162 A-1 was ready on 25 March 1945. It was built by the Heinkel works at Marienehe.

Opposite page, bottom: During the first part of the He 162 flight evaluation three pilots crashed. *Flugkapitän* Dipl.-Ing. Gotthold Peter (here in the cockpit) was killed in the first prototype on 10 December 1944. On 4 February 1945 *Oberleutnant* Wedemeyer's He 162 M6 was lost, followed by *Flugzeugbaumeister* Full's He 162 M2 on 25 February 1945 while testing an enlarged fin section. The Heinkel works also reported other, lesser, damages during the testing phase.

Below: The *Erprobungskommando* 162 at Ludwigslust. On 1 January 1945 EK 162 was established by the *Generalquartiermeister* of the *Luftwaffe*, with the principal aim of allowing *Luftwaffe* pilots to test the new jet fighter. On 25 February 1945 the OKL ordered it to raise a first operational *Gruppe*, the I./*Jagdgeschwader* 1. The unit was sent to Parchim to take over the first '*Volksjäger*' in March 1945. The first series He 162 was not available until 1 April 1945.

Right: A front view of one of the new Heinkel jet fighters being delivered to *Jagdgeschwader* 1 'Oesau' at Ludwigslust. The first *Gruppe* of JG 1 was stationed there in April 1945 while the second one was due to be based at Garz. Lack of fuel made the jet pilots' training phase very short and caused further losses. The commanding officer of II./JG 1, Knight's Cross holder *Hauptmann* Paul H. Dähne, was killed during a training flight.

Opposite page, bottom: Lined up at Leck in Schleswig-Holstein, the He 162s of *Einsatzgruppe Jagdgeschwader* 1 await the arrival of British soldiers after news of the unconditional surrender. The explosive loads had been removed from the aircraft the previous night, by the order of the commanding officer *Oberstleutnant* Herbert Ihlefeld. At that time the entire *Jagdgeschwader* comprised just two *Einsatz-Staffeln*.

Opposite page, top: Another view of the He 162s at Leck. During the last days of the War little flight action had been reported. A few pilots had been ordered to shoot down British piston fighter-bombers over the Flensburg–Heide–Schleswig region since 25 April 1945. They were also ordered to intercept DH Mosquitos which operated over northern Germany.

Left: A few days earlier, *Leutnant* R. Schmitt had damaged an RAF fighter in action; now the *Luftwaffe* officers looked back on a lost war and contemplated new professions. Here in front of their former fighters are (left to right) *Major* Zober, *Oberleutnant* Demuth and *Hauptmann* Künnecke.

Above: This He 162 A-2 was one of those handed over to the RAF for flight evaluation. Two of the 'Volksjäger' could be transported without wings and fin sections on captured *Reichsbahn* twin-bogie flatcars. The *Geschwader*, *Gruppe* and *Staffel* emblems have been painted on the side of this aircraft's fuselage.

Above: In 1944 Allied air raids made it necessary to disperse all major aircraft factories across the country. Key industries were also moved into the natural or artificial caverns of former mining companies. At Mödling, near Vienna, an underground factory called 'Languste' had been established in this way. He 162 fuselages and wings could be transported on little trolleys through this narrow drift.

Left: A view into the underground production site at Mödling. Slave labourers had to construct wooden spare parts for the *'Volksjäger'* programme on these wooden working tables. After German forces retreated the underground factory was destroyed by its own personnel. Most of the assembled He 162s were flown to Linz and then to Memmingen.

Opposite page: A couple of these training systems were constructed to teach *'Volksjäger'* pilots to handle the propulsion, since they were familiar only with the flight behaviour of piston engines. The static training rig presented the main instruments of the He 162 A aircraft and the BMW 003 turbo-jet. A glider conversion of the *'Volksjäger'*, without propulsion, was proposed for actual flight training.

Above: Members of the ground crew of *Jagdgeschwader* 1 work on an early He 162 A-2 jet fighter on 15 May 1945. Under *Oberleutnant* Wolfgang Wollenweber's supervision the men prepare the jet fighter carrying a 'White 3', still armed with two 20 mm guns, for future flight training of RAF pilots. At that time most of the crews were in a camp near Schmörholm, from which most of the former JG 1 officers were discharged early in July 1945.

Below: Most of the airworthy He 162s like this one were captured by British ground forces at Leck; some others were found by American soldiers in the Kassel region and at Munich-Riem. Soviet troops also found several aircraft in central Germany, where the He 162 was constructed by Heinkel, Junkers and the Mittelwerke.